THINGS EVERY KID SHOULD KNOW ABOUT GOD

Discover Who God Is, Grow Your Faith, Experience His Love, and Live with Purpose! (Christian Book for Kids)

ALEX HAYNES

FREE BONUS

SCAN TO GET OUR NEXT BOOK FOR FREE!

Table of Contents

INTRODUCTION

Welcome to the beginning of *Things Every Kid Should Know About God*. You're probably reading this book because you have questions about God, your faith, and what it means to be a Christian. It's normal to be curious about your religion and God's role in the world around you.

Together, we'll explore more about God as a loving Father, friend, and shepherd. You'll learn all about the story of creation and how humans first came to exist. In later chapters, we'll talk about how to see God in everyday life and live according to His teachings.

This guide will help you build a stronger relationship with God as you discover more about prayer, forgiveness, and acts of service. You'll also learn about spiritual growth and how to inspire other people with your faith. You don't have to wait until you're an adult to help your community or be more active in your church.

This might seem like a lot of information, but there's no reason to rush through it. Take your time with each section, and don't hesitate to bring up topics with your loved ones or leaders in your church. They'll be able to answer any extra questions you may have or tell you how to find out more about something you read about in one of these chapters.

The important thing is that you're curious and willing to learn. Many Christians continue to study the Bible and ask questions about God for their entire lives. There's so much to understand, and some people disagree about certain topics. In some cases, you'll need to form your own opinions and decide what you think is right based on your personal relationship with God.

CHAPTER ONE:
WHO IS GOD?

God is the creator of everything you see around you. From the stars to the oceans, God designed each part of the world. He has many attributes, but He's known for being loving, kind, and forgiving. Even though you can't see God the way you visit with your family or friends, He's always there watching over you.

UNDERSTANDING THE CONCEPT OF GOD

It isn't possible to fully understand everything about God. He's so powerful and knows so much about the universe that we won't ever have the chance to discover for ourselves. That's why it's important to trust God and have faith in Him, even if it seems like the world is a confusing or stressful place.

The Holy Trinity: Father, Son, and Holy Spirit

There is only one God in Christianity, but you might also hear about the Holy Trinity. The Holy Trinity describes the three different forms of God. If that sounds confusing, think about a single tree with three branches. Each branch is part of the same tree, but they're also separate from each other. Similarly, God is three different forms in one:

The first person in the Holy Trinity is God the Father. In His role as creator, God is like a father to us all. He loves us even though we sin or break the rules.

The second person is God the Son. God sent Jesus Christ, His only Son, to save humanity from sin. In other words, Jesus Christ is the human form of God who came to live among us and teach humans how to honor God.

The third person is the Holy Spirit. The Holy Spirit is how God continues to do His work on Earth. The power of the Holy Spirit allows God to guide us even though He isn't physically here to talk to us.

ATTRIBUTES OF GOD

God has many qualities that are described to us in the Bible. He is loving and merciful toward humanity, but He's also aware of our weaknesses. As humans, we can't fully understand every attribute of God since we don't have the same power, wisdom, and all-knowing nature.

Loving and Kind

God loves all of us as His children. In Isaiah 54:10, the Lord says, "…my unfailing love for you will not be shaken." As the one who created us, God knows us on a deep level. He understands our needs, talents, fears, and dreams for the future. No matter what happens, He's there to listen and support us through life.

God is also kind and forgiving. He doesn't expect people to be perfect, and He's willing to forgive us when we've made the wrong decisions. God's kindness should inspire you to be kind to others in your life.

Powerful and Wise

When you read stories in the Bible, you'll realize that God sometimes gets angry or upset with His followers. Even though He's powerful enough to punish sinners who don't follow His teachings, God is also patient and wise. He understands that ordinary people make mistakes, and He's forgiving when we admit that we didn't make the right decisions.

Eternal, Unchanging, and All-Knowing

God has watched over all of creation since the beginning of the universe. He knows everything that's happened and everything that could happen in the future. This knowledge gives Him a point of view that we can't understand as ordinary people.

Sometimes, it can be tough to understand certain events. Maybe a bad thing had to happen to a good person in order to carry out God's plan. It doesn't necessarily make sense to us, but we can't always see the bigger picture. In those situations, you need to trust the all-knowing nature of God and that everything in life has a greater purpose.

NAMES AND TITLES
OF GOD

God is known by many different names. Each of these words is used to describe a different aspect of God's identity. It's just like saying someone is a friend and a classmate. They're both those things at once, but each role they play is a little different.

Lord and Creator, Father and Shepherd

God rules over everything you see around you. As the creator of the universe, He is the Lord of the heavens and the Earth. We worship Him to show our appreciation for everything we have on Earth.

However, it's also important to have a closer connection with God. He isn't a distant power who made the Earth and left us alone. God teaches and guides us just like a father. When someone strays away from the right path, God is a shepherd who shows them how to return.

HOW CHRISTIANS
VIEW GOD

Christians believe that God is always present and aware of what's happening in the world. Following God's laws and avoiding sin are just two of the ways that Christians honor their faith. The Bible helps us learn about God and understand more about His wishes.

God as a Loving Father and Friend

God watches over us and offers His love and friendship. It's up to us to accept God's friendship by speaking to Him through prayer and following the rules we read about in the Bible. After all, you wouldn't want to stay friends with someone if they didn't respect your boundaries or spend time with you.

God is always there to accept us when we're ready. Even if you didn't used to believe in God, it doesn't mean you can't reconnect now or in the future. Some people take years and years to hear God calling out to them. God is patient and understanding in these moments. All you need to do is reach out.

CHAPTER TWO: GOD'S CREATION

Everything around us was once fresh and new. God is eternal and has been watching over the Earth since He first created it. Over the years, society has changed and grown, but we're all still part of God's plan for the universe.

THE STORY OF CREATION

You've probably already heard the story of how God created the heavens and the Earth. After all, it's one of the most famous stories ever told. In the book of Genesis, we learn that God created the universe in seven days. Here's what He made on each day:

- Day 1: light and darkness
- Day 2: sky
- Day 3: land, sea, plants, and trees
- Day 4: sun and moon
- Day 5: animals of the air and sea
- Day 6: animals of the land and humans

When God made humans, He started with Adam. One by one, He brought the animals to Adam and let him name them. But even though God had made many creatures, Adam was lonely. God decided that Adam needed a companion. He took one of Adam's ribs and made it into Eve.

Once God's work was done, He blessed the seventh day and used it for rest. After that, the seventh day of the week became known as the *Sabbath*. Christians honor God by keeping the Sabbath holy, which is also one of the Ten Commandments.

The Tree of the Knowledge of Good and Evil

God is generous, so when He made Adam, He told him that he could eat almost any fruit in the Garden of Eden. It was only forbidden to eat from the Tree of the Knowledge of Good and Evil. After God made Eve, Adam taught her the same lesson. It was one of God's first tests to see if Adam and Eve would follow His rules.

However, Satan was hiding in the garden in the form of a snake. He told Eve that nothing bad would happen to her if she ate from the forbidden tree. She ate the fruit and shared some with Adam. They immediately became aware that they were naked and covered themselves. When God noticed, He realized they had eaten from the Tree of the Knowledge of Good and Evil. As punishment, God banished Adam and Eve from the garden.

THE PURPOSE OF CREATION

When you think about the world, it's clear that everything and everyone has a purpose. The sun provides us with light and warmth, while the rain gives us the water we need to survive. Without these basic parts of God's design, nothing on Earth would be able to live. When you think about how all these different things work together, it isn't difficult to see that they were designed by a powerful, all-knowing God.

Why God Created the World

God created the world because He wanted other creatures to share in His glory and experience life. This gave Him the opportunity to share his love and wisdom. He also gave humans free will instead of designing us to only follow His instructions.

God didn't want us to be like robots that He could order around. Free will gives us the ability to choose God and love Him because it's what we want to do. We can use our spirituality and our intelligence to make our own decisions about God. That's something unique that sets us apart from animals.

Follow God's teachings because it's our choice makes our relationship with God even stronger. Just think of the other people in your life. If someone is only your friend because they're forced to hang out with you, the situation doesn't seem very fair to that person. On the other hand, if they choose to spend time with you because they like who you are as a person, then it feels real.

THE BEAUTY OF
THE NATURAL WORLD

We're still learning everything there is to know about the world. Scientists continue to make discoveries about the Earth, natural phenomena, and everyday creatures. Studying the natural world helps us appreciate all that God has made.

Seeing God in Nature

It isn't hard to see God when you look at the beauty and complexity of nature. The next time you watch a dog playing or notice a bee buzzing around a flower, just think of how many different creatures there are around us. Every animal or insect has its own set of instincts that trace back to how it was originally designed by God.

Thinking about how God made each creature can also make school more interesting as you learn about different plants and animals. Imagine how much effort went into making each living thing you hear about. From zebras to roses, God's creativity is amazing.

HUMANS AS PART OF GOD'S CREATION

Just like God created animals, He also created humans. As you've already learned, the first humans were Adam and Eve. Now, all these years later, there are almost eight billion people living on the planet. A lot has obviously changed since the time of Adam and Eve, but we can still try to live according to our original purpose from God.

Created in God's Image

Of every creature in the natural world, humans are the only ones made in God's image. This doesn't mean that we physically look like God. Humans share God's image in a spiritual sense because we're able to think, make choices, and try to be good people. Animals don't have this same ability, which makes humans special.

Taking Care of the Natural World

Besides caring about other people, we also need to think about the living creatures around us. When God made humans, He gave us the responsibility of working the land and taking care of it. It's our job to watch over the planet and look after everything that God has made.

In daily life, taking care of the natural world could involve helping animals, recycling, or only buying products that are good for the Earth. When we respect the planet, we respect God's creation and fulfill one of our earliest responsibilities as humans.

CHAPTER THREE:
TALKING TO GOD
PRAYER

Prayer is a major part of being a Christian. In simple terms, it's how we talk to God. It's how we share our thoughts, praise Him, and give thanks for our blessings. Praying also creates time and space for us to listen to God in return. Even though He doesn't speak to us directly, praying shows that you're open to God's guidance and thinking about how to live according to His rules.

TALKING TO GOD LIKE A FRIEND

God knows and loves you just the way you are, so don't be afraid to talk to Him like a friend. It isn't wrong or disrespectful to have a regular conversation with God during prayer. It just shows that you're comfortable in your relationship with God and willing to open up about your true feelings.

Being honest is important. There's no need to be embarrassed or try to hide your thoughts from God. Instead, think of God like a friend who's there to support you no matter what. Sharing what you're thinking and experiencing is a way of welcoming God into your daily life.

DIFFERENT WAYS TO PRAY

Christianity includes many different branches, known as *denominations*. For example, Catholics and Lutherans are both

Christians, but they have certain unique beliefs that set them apart. The prayers you hear in church might be different from the prayers used in other churches depending on the denomination you follow.

No matter how you pray, all Christians are still speaking to the same God. In addition to special prayers that are said the same way every time, you can also pray in your own words. Even if you're not sure exactly what to say, the important thing is that you're taking the time to connect with God.

Prayers of Thanks and Asking

There are many reasons to pray and open yourself up to God. God is always ready to listen, so don't worry if you want to talk to Him about something that seems minor. Not every prayer has to be about a serious concern. For example, you might want to say a prayer of thanks because you had time after school to watch your favorite movie. This just shows that you appreciate the blessings in your everyday life.

You might also pray to ask God to help you with a problem or guide you through a tough decision. Talking through the situation with God can make it easier for you to see the right path forward. If you're worried about embarrassing yourself during your piano recital, you could pray to God to ask Him to give you confidence in your skills.

When you pray to God for help, remember to be humble and only ask for things you truly need. It isn't appropriate to ask for favors like finding money. Praying is about strengthening your relationship with God, not about personal gain.

Prayers for Others

A simple way to remember to pray for others is by using the Five Finger Prayer. Each finger represents a different person to pray for. This can help you keep track of your prayers and remind you to think of others.

Start with your thumb. This finger is for the people who are the closest to you. Family, friends, and other loved ones fall into this group. You can pray for something specific, such as a family member getting better after feeling sick, or you can just ask God to protect your loved ones.

Your pointer finger is next. Use this time to pray for people who guide you and point you in the right direction. Maybe you're especially thankful that a teacher took the time to work through a problem with you at school, or maybe you had a great conversation with your pastor after church. Praying for them is a way to show appreciation and thank God for putting those people in your path.

Your middle finger is for people in leadership. You might say a prayer asking God to help them make the right decisions as they lead the government. This part of your prayer could include praying for protection to ensure other authority figures, such as military personnel, stay safe.

Your ring finger is for people who feel weak or lost. Say a prayer for those struggling to get through a tough time. Ask God to give them the strength to keep going even if they're dealing with challenges like health problems or poverty.

Lastly, your pinky finger is for yourself. The pinky is your littlest finger and the last one on your hand. This exercise encourages you to think about other people before you concentrate on your own needs.

Special Prayers to Memorize

You might already have some prayers memorized, especially if you recite them in church week after week. For example, you may know the Lord's Prayer. This prayer is used to honor God, ask for forgiveness, and help us avoid the temptation of evil.

The prayers you learn by heart may also vary based on where you attend church. Catholics pray to the Virgin Mary and the saints, but some other types of Christians don't. If you're Catholic, you'll learn to say special prayers, such as the Hail Mary, that aren't used in all other denominations.

Praying the Rosary

Rosaries are most commonly used by Catholics. A rosary is a string of beads to count the number of prayers you've said. Praying the Rosary has to be done in order. Don't worry if you don't know how to say this set of prayers on your own. Many kids need to practice

and follow along with others before fully understanding this
method of praying.

PRAYER IN
DAILY LIFE

Praying can quickly become a regular part of your routine. Setting
aside time to pray throughout the day shows that you're thinking
about God and making space for Him even when you're busy with
school, sports, or other activities.

You don't need to go to church to pray. You can pray almost
anywhere as long as you have a few minutes to yourself. If you're
not sure how to make prayer part of your daily life, talk to your
loved ones or other people in your church to see when they pray
throughout the day.

Making Prayer a Habit

Choosing a specific time to pray can help you make prayer a habit.
It's common to pray at night before you go to sleep. This way, you
can reflect on everything that happened and talk through any
important issues with God. Some people also enjoy praying in the
morning to start their day by honoring God. It's up to you and
what feels best.

Don't worry about how long you're praying. You might only pray
for a short time one day but have a much longer prayer session
later in the week. God doesn't set a timer to grade you on how long

you pray. The most important thing is that you're making an effort to connect with Him in your everyday life.

Even after you pick a schedule for your daily prayers, you can still pray at other times. For example, many people pray before they eat a meal to offer thanks. You may also want to pray more when you're worried or looking for guidance.

If you miss a day because you forgot to pray or your schedule got busier than expected, you can still get right back into your routine the next day. Don't worry about God being angry with you. He won't tune you out just because you haven't prayed in a while. If you're nervous or guilty, simply talk through it with God and explain your feelings.

Praying Together

If your friends or family members also pray, try to make time to pray together. Some groups gather in the same place but say their own separate prayers in their heads. Other groups follow along as one person prays out loud and serves as a leader.

Rotating who says a prayer out loud is a great way to practice worshipping with other people. It also gives you a chance to choose what you want to talk about with God and share your thoughts with your loved ones. If you know it's your turn to lead a prayer; you can also find passages from the Bible to read together before praying.

CHAPTER FOUR: LEARNING ABOUT GOD

There's so much to learn and understand about God. One of the best ways to study on your own is by reading the Bible. You can read it in order or look up a particular section if there's something special you want to know.

Since the Bible was written long ago, some of the stories or words might be confusing. It can help to get a children's version of the Bible that explains events in simpler language. Many children's Bibles include illustrations to show you what life might have been like during various stories.

RELIGIOUS TEXTS AND SCRIPTURES

Most religions have some type of holy text or scripture. In Christianity, we rely on the Bible, which is divided into two parts: the Old Testament and the New Testament. You may also see slightly different versions of the Bible based on how they were translated. The New International Version and the King James Version of the Bible are especially popular.

The Bible: Old Testament

The Old Testament is divided into multiple parts that are known as *books*. Protestant Bibles have 39 books in the Old Testament, while Catholic Bibles may have up to 46. The Hebrew Bible also contains the same 39 books as the Old Testament, which is why Jews and Christians have some shared beliefs.

This section of the Bible focuses on the creation of the universe and how humans broke God's trust by believing Satan in the Garden of Eden. Christians believe that the Old Testament predicts the coming of Jesus Christ as a savior and Messiah. For example, Isaiah 9:6 states, "For unto us a child is born, unto us a Son is given, and the government will be upon His shoulders. And He will be called Wonderful Counselor, Mighty God, Everlasting Father, Prince of Peace."

The Bible: New Testament

The New Testament is made up of 27 books. It also includes four different gospels written by Matthew, Mark, Luke, and John. This part of the Bible is about how Jesus Christ the Messiah saved humanity by dying for our sins. It describes the main events of His life and how He shared the message of God's love.

Jews don't believe that Jesus is the Messiah predicted by prophets such as Isaiah and Ezekiel. That's why they only follow the Old Testament, not the New Testament.

STORIES AND PARABLES ABOUT GOD

Parables are stories about ordinary life that teach us a spiritual lesson. Jesus often shared parables with His followers. His stories focused on everyday situations and problems that were familiar to many people. Parables made it easier for people to learn more about God by comparing parts of Christianity to things they already understood.

Not everyone agrees on the number of parables in the Bible. Some stories might count as parables to one group but not to another. Most people believe that there are at least 30 parables spread throughout the gospels of Matthew, Mark, and Luke. Certain versions of the Bible also have lists of Jesus's parables and where to find them.

The Prodigal Son

Some parables are more famous than others. Even people who aren't Christians are usually familiar with at least a few of these stories from the Bible. One of the most well-known parables is "The Prodigal Son" from the gospel of Luke.

In this parable, a father has two sons with different opinions about how to live. The older son is respectful and works hard to honor his father. The younger son wants to go off on his own, so he asks for his portion of his inheritance even though his father is still alive. The father agrees and gives the money to his younger son.

Later on, there's a famine. Since the younger son already lost his inheritance, he ends up having to work for a pig farmer. He realizes that he made a terrible mistake leaving home and decides to go back and ask for his father's forgiveness. His father welcomes him home and gives him special gifts.

Meanwhile, the older son is upset that his father is celebrating the younger son. In his eyes, the older son is more deserving of gifts since he stayed home and worked hard for the family while the younger son was disrespectful.

This parable has many different lessons. Overall, it's meant to show that God welcomes us back even when we've made bad decisions or hurt those around us. It reminds us that we can always ask for God's forgiveness and love. Instead of focusing on things we did wrong in the past, God wants us to look forward to a better future as part of His family.

"The Prodigal Son" also warns against expecting others to be perfect. The older son should have been happy to see his brother instead of feeling like he was better or superior. At the end of the story, the father talks with his older son and says, "Son, you have always been with me, and all that is mine is yours. But we had to celebrate and rejoice, for this brother of yours was dead and has begun to live, and was lost and has been found."

The Lost Sheep

Another well-known parable is "The Lost Sheep." It appears in the gospels of Matthew and Luke. Jesus is speaking to a group of sinners and asks them to imagine that one of them has 100 sheep. One of the sheep wanders off and gets lost. Instead of just accepting that the sheep is gone, the shepherd leaves the group of 99 sheep and searches for the missing one until he finds it. He brings it back to his flock and celebrates that they're reunited.

This simple parable teaches the sinners that they matter just as much as other people who have never wandered away from God. It shows that God is always willing to celebrate Christians who return no matter why they left or how long they were lost. "The Lost Sheep" also tells us that God continues to search for lost sinners while they're away from the flock.

HOW TO STUDY AND UNDERSTAND THE BIBLE

Studying the Bible is different from studying other subjects. It isn't like math, where you can learn how to solve certain problems and move on. Even if you've already read the Bible, you should still talk about it with others and revisit the most important lessons. You never know when a sermon at church will inspire you to study a different book of the Bible or share your thoughts with loved ones.

Plus, your understanding of the Bible will most likely change as you get older and experience more of the world. After all, you probably don't have the same opinions you did when you were five or six years old. Studying the Bible as you grow can help you see different points of view that you might have missed in the past.

Bible Study

Bible study groups meet to discuss different parts of the Bible. Most churches have some sort of youth group or Bible study for kids on a regular basis. Ask your parents or guardians about signing up. Bible study gives you the chance to share your thoughts and discuss ideas with other kids.

Some families also decide to have Bible study on their own; this doesn't have to be limited to your immediate family. Maybe your grandparents or cousins want to join in, too. If you don't all live in the same area, you might be able to have a virtual Bible study online.

Sunday School and Small Groups

Sunday school is another chance to learn more about the Bible. Many churches offer classes for different age groups. These short classes give you the chance to become more involved in your church and meet other kids your age.

Some churches also have small groups that meet on their own schedule. Small groups have fewer people than a whole class, so it's easier for everyone to share and participate. Small groups can be divided by age or centered around shared hobbies like doing arts and crafts. If you have an idea for a small group that doesn't exist yet, talk to your church leaders about starting your own.

THE ROLE OF RELIGIOUS TEACHERS AND LEADERS

Pastors, Sunday school teachers, and other religious leaders are there to help if you need extra spiritual support. You can go to them for advice or ask them questions about something you read in the Bible. Their role isn't to judge you, so don't feel embarrassed about talking to them one-on-one.

Religious leaders want to see you succeed and be at peace with God. In fact, a lot of leaders are volunteers who give back to the church because they want to honor God and help the community. You aren't bothering them by asking for a little bit of their time. Even if they don't know how to solve your problem, they can pray with you or suggest readings from the Bible.

Religious leaders can also help you prepare for big events in your life as a Christian. For example, kids often have questions about their First Communion or first confession. Having extra support makes it easier to get ready and learn everything you'll need to know for special occasions.

Leaders in the Church

Besides the leaders in your church, there are also leaders who help guide entire denominations. The Pope is the overall head of the Catholic Church. His role is to answer religious questions, appoint bishops, and decide on official policies for Catholics. The Pope lives in Vatican City, which is its own separate state inside of Rome.

Denominations that aren't Catholic don't follow the Pope. For example, the Patriarch of All Romania is the head of the Romanian Orthodox Church. In general, each branch of Christianity has its own separate leaders. If you aren't sure who leads your denomination, ask for more information the next time you're at church.

CHAPTER FIVE:
GOD'S LOVE AND
KINDNESS

As our creator, God's love for us is more powerful and unique than any other kind of love. God designed each of us and knows us better than any other person ever could. Ephesians 3:19 says, "May you experience the love of Christ, though it is too great to understand fully. Then you will be made complete with all the fullness of life and power that comes from God."

GOD'S LOVE SHOWN THROUGH JESUS

God's greatest act of love was to send Jesus to pay for the sins of humanity. John 3:16 says, "For God so loved the world, that He gave His only begotten Son, that whosoever believeth in Him should not perish, but have everlasting life." When Adam and Eve ate the forbidden fruit, they broke their word to God. Jesus fixed the relationship between humans and God when He died for our sins.

God even shares His love with people who don't believe in Him. Anyone can embrace Jesus and the Lord at any time. By offering forgiveness, God gives all sinners a chance to accept Him regardless of what they might have said or done in the past.

STORIES OF
GOD'S LOVE

We've already talked about a few stories like "The Lost Sheep" that show God's love for all His children. There are dozens of other examples throughout the Bible. One method of finding stories about God's love is to read the Bible while focusing on that theme.

This is a little different from reading the Bible in general. During a themed reading, you're looking for any stories that relate to God's love. Not all of them will be obvious. When you revisit your favorite stories, you might notice details you missed before or realize that God's love is shining through in a unique way.

Besides reading the Bible, you can also find real-life stories of God's love just by listening to other people. The next time someone talks about something wonderful that happened to them or shares how prayer inspired them to make the right choices, take a moment to think about how God improved their life. These stories remind us that God blesses us every day.

SHOWING LOVE
AND KINDNESS
TO OTHERS

There are many ways to show love for others. From baking cookies for your brother's birthday to complimenting your friend's dress, you can find opportunities to be kind in almost any situation. You should also try to be kind to strangers you meet while going about your daily life. Maybe you have a substitute teacher who seems frazzled at the start of class. If they seem confused or disorganized, ask if they need help. You might know where to find what they're looking for.

It's also important to have kind thoughts about others, even if they'll never know what you really think about them. The people you see in the world have their own lives, beliefs, and interests that won't always match up with yours. If you notice yourself having an unkind thought about someone, stop and work through it in your head. Why did you have that thought?

For example, you might think something unkind because you're actually jealous. In that case, you need to work on jealousy *and* showing love to others. Being honest with yourself can help you grow and see where you're straying away from God's teachings.

Loving Your Neighbor

Loving your neighbor is about treating others with respect, kindness, and understanding. Showing love could involve helping someone in your community or making friends with the new kid in your class. The important part is to love everyone, not just the people you know best or who are most like you. Ephesians 5:2 says, "And walk in the way of love, just as Christ loved us and gave himself up for us as a fragrant offering and sacrifice to God."

Loving Your Enemies

In Matthew 5:43–45, Jesus states, "You have heard that it was said, 'Love your neighbor and hate your enemy.' But I tell you, love your enemies and pray for those who persecute you, that you may be children of your Father in heaven."

Instead of reacting with hate or anger, Jesus teaches us to show love even when others aren't kind to us. Loving your enemies isn't easy, and many adults still have trouble forgiving the people who have hurt them in the past. If you're having trouble loving your enemies, just remember that Jesus always encouraged everyone to put more love into the world.

In the Sermon on the Mount, Jesus reminds us that even God shows kindness to people who speak out against Him. "He causes His sun to rise on the evil and the good and sends rain on the righteous and the unrighteous."

THE IMPORTANCE OF FORGIVENESS

Forgiveness is a choice you make to avoid letting negative emotions take over. Imagine that you caught one of your friends spreading rumors about you and making fun of you behind your back. Every time you see them on the bus, you feel like yelling at them and telling them how much they hurt you. Having to be around them ruins your whole morning, and you end up being grumpy all the way until lunch.

While that's understandable, it doesn't have to continue that way. When you forgive someone, you let go of all the anger and pain you're feeling toward that person. It can be healing to move on. Instead of focusing on the bad that happened, you can think back to good times or look forward to a better future.

Forgiving Others as God Forgives Us

Knowing that God won't abandon us for making a mistake allows us to fully experience His love. Even when God banished Adam and Eve from the Garden of Eden, He didn't turn His back on them forever. We can learn from God's forgiveness and mercy by forgiving others.

Remember that forgiveness doesn't mean you have to excuse another person's behavior. God still banished Adam and Eve even though He forgave them later. You always have the option to avoid people who haven't been kind to you.

CHAPTER SIX: LIVING A GODLY LIFE

Living a godly life requires us to put God's teachings above our own wants and the Earthly world. When you're fully dedicated to God, you realize that being successful in human society comes second. You should still work hard to get good grades and do your best at activities, but don't become so distracted that you start to forget about your responsibilities to God.

LIVING ACCORDING TO GOD'S TEACHINGS

Living according to God's teachings is a choice. When you need to make a decision, it's up to you to pick the right path. Society has changed since the Bible was written, and you won't always find an obvious answer.

Two Christians may have completely opposite opinions about a problem or situation. In the end, you have to do what you feel is closest to God's teachings. Others might not agree with your choices, but that's why we all have our own personal relationships with God.

The Ten Commandments

The Ten Commandments are God's laws that tell us how to live. They date back to the time of Moses when he led the Israelites out of Egypt and across the Red Sea. Eventually, they came to Mount Sinai. Moses climbed the mountain to receive God's instructions. God gave him two stone tablets engraved with the Ten

Commandments. You can read the full version in Exodus 20 and Deuteronomy 5.

Since God didn't number the Ten Commandments, different churches have their own versions. Most Protestant and Orthodox churches use this format:

1. Thou shalt have no other gods before me.
2. Thou shalt not make unto thee any graven image.
3. Thou shalt not take the name of the Lord thy God in vain.
4. Remember the Sabbath day to keep it holy.
5. Honor thy father and thy mother.
6. Thou shalt not kill.
7. Thou shalt not commit adultery.
8. Thou shalt not steal.
9. Thou shalt not bear false witness against thy neighbor.
10. Thou shalt not covet thy neighbor's house (or anything that belongs to your neighbor).

The version used by the Catholic Church doesn't include the commandment about graven images and changes "Sabbath day" to "the Lord's Day." It also has two commandments about coveting someone else:

9. You shall not covet your neighbor's wife.
10. You shall not covet anything that belongs to your neighbor.

HONESTY, KINDNESS, AND RESPECT

Honesty, kindness, and respect are three of the most important Christian values. Living by these values means stopping to think about how God would want you to act in any situation. For example, if a kid in your neighborhood is mean to you for no reason, that isn't an excuse to say hurtful things back. You should always try to show kindness first. You don't know what other people are going through or whether they're just having a bad day.

However, you also can't control how other people react. If it gets to the point that someone is bullying you, it's always okay to tell an adult. Living by Christian values doesn't mean that you can't stand up for yourself. The key is to lead with love whenever possible and forgive people even when they don't return your kindness.

MAKING GOOD CHOICES AND HELPING OTHERS

Part of making good choices is thinking about how they affect other people. The actions and decisions that are best for you won't necessarily benefit the entire group. If you eat all the cake at a party, no one else can enjoy dessert. You wouldn't want someone else to behave that way, so you shouldn't either.

It's also important to remember that you can have good intentions but still hurt others by accident. Imagine playing a prank on your friend because you think it'll be funny. Instead, you end up scaring them. Even though you just wanted to make them laugh, your good intentions don't change the fact that your friend is upset.

Being able to think through what might happen can help you make better decisions in the future. If you know there's a chance that one of your choices might hurt someone else's feelings, you can pick a different option.

Giving Generously

Helping others may involve giving money or items away. Showing charity toward the less fortunate is a way of honoring God by sharing your blessings. Being generous is about giving away more than just things you don't want or need anymore. While donating unwanted clothes or toys will still help others, it doesn't show that you have a giving spirit.

A story from Mark 12:41–12:44 teaches us an important lesson about generosity. Jesus went to Jerusalem and watched people giving money to the temple. Rich people gave large amounts without a thought. A poor widow, on the other hand, only gave two of the smallest coins. Jesus turned to his disciples and told them that the widow was more generous than any of the others. The rich people gave because they didn't need the money to live, but the widow gave money even though she was poor.

Volunteering

Volunteering allows you to help others by being generous with your time. Ask your Sunday school teacher or another leader about any kid-friendly programs you can join. Your church probably has tons of events where you can volunteer to set up tables, clean up, or hang up decorations.

You may also want to volunteer with a club or a local organization. The cause you choose doesn't necessarily have to be religious as long as you feel like it's still helping you live according to God's teachings. For instance, if you love animals, volunteering at a rescue gives you the chance to take care of God's creatures.

STAYING HUMBLE

Being humble is about recognizing that everyone has their own skills and talents. You might be talented at certain things, but that doesn't mean you're better than anyone else overall. Even Jesus's disciples needed to be reminded of this lesson.

During Jesus's time, people wore sandals and picked up dirt from the road as they walked. Before eating together, servants would wash the feet of any guests. Since there weren't any servants present at the Last Supper, Jesus washed his disciples' feet to show humility.

The disciples had just been arguing about which of them was the best. Jesus washing their feet showed them they needed to be humble instead of bragging or feeling superior. It also taught them the importance of serving and supporting other people.

Think about this story whenever you feel better than those around you. For example, you might be the top player on your soccer team. Instead of showing off, use your skills to help others learn and get better. Encouraging kids who aren't as skilled shows that you're a team player and care about everyone as a group instead of just your own reputation.

CHAPTER SEVEN: GOD IN EVERYDAY LIFE

God is all around us if you just know where to look. You don't have to go to church to feel His presence or see that His work is being carried out in the world. Just think about your best friends. Aren't they amazing? Not only is it wonderful that God created such awesome people, but it's also incredible that they're part of your life. Your paths lined up perfectly so that you'd meet and become friends.

Sometimes, it's tough to take a step back from everything else going on in your life. If you're worried about your audition for the school play or studying hard for a test, that can take up all your brain power if you let it. Making prayer part of your routine will remind you to think of God and your spiritual needs even when you're busy.

RECOGNIZING BLESSINGS AND EXPRESSING GRATITUDE

Once you learn how to see God in daily experiences, you'll start to notice how He blesses us in small ways every day. Writing in a journal can help you get in the habit of expressing thanks for these moments. Every afternoon or evening, write down a few positive things that happened. Maybe you had the chance to go out to your favorite restaurant or spend time with your best friend at recess.

When you say your prayers, think back to what you wrote and thank God for each of your blessings. Talking about what you're thankful for in detail shows that you're truly paying attention to all that God has done for you.

Saying Grace

Saying grace before eating is a simple way of showing gratitude to God. It thanks Him for providing what we need to survive. There isn't a specific prayer that everyone says before eating. If you visit a friend's house, they might have a totally different way of saying grace than what you're used to at home. For most people, it's common to use a shorter prayer unless it's a special occasion or a major holiday. For example, you might say, "God is great, and God is good. Let us thank Him for this food. Amen."

Taking turns saying grace allows everyone to have the chance to lead. Even if you're nervous about talking in front of your loved ones, learning how to praise God in public is an important part of your journey as a Christian. You can either memorize a prayer in advance or come up with something on the spot based on how you feel.

Celebrating Talents

God's gifts aren't always physical. Your talents and skills are also part of God's gifts to you. Everyone has natural skills and talents that shine through. Some people are great at sports, while others are amazing at playing musical instruments. Think of a few of your talents that make you proud. You've probably put in a lot of hard work and effort to make your skills even better than they were before. That's definitely something to celebrate.

At the same time, you should also thank God for giving you those natural abilities in the first place. He designed you with those talents and put you on a path where you could discover them for yourself. Appreciating God's role in your achievements shows humility and respect for His plan.

You should also celebrate other people's talents. If someone cooks you a delicious meal or teaches you a new skill, they're sharing their talents from God. Seeing God at work in your friends, loved ones, or even total strangers is a powerful experience. It's proof that each of us is unique and made with care.

FINDING PEACE AND COMFORT IN GOD

God is always listening. It can be comforting to know that all you need to do is reach out in prayer for Him to hear you. If you're upset or don't feel like anyone is paying attention to what you need, God is there for you.

As our creator, He knows us better than anyone else ever could. He already knows your flaws and any mistakes you might have made, but He loves you anyway. You don't need to hide from God, especially when feeling lost or confused.

Finding God in Nature

Many people turn to nature when they want to be closer to God. Being outside in the trees and the grass can remind you that we're surrounded by God's creation. Even if you live in a busy city that doesn't have a lot of nature, you can always find a park or look up at the sky to feel closer to God.

You can even go outside to pray if you feel more at home in nature. Find a peaceful spot in your yard or ask if you can go for a short walk. Being in the fresh air can help you clear your mind and open yourself to God.

TRUSTING GOD IN DIFFICULT TIMES

It isn't always easy to trust God, and it's okay to admit when you're having a hard time believing that everything will work out. In fact, you can even pray about it and share your thoughts with God. You might say, "God, I don't understand why this is happening. I trust You, but I'm scared about the future."

In that example, you're showing God that you still trust Him even though you're afraid. The real issue is your fear of uncertainty, not your faith in God. Sharing your experiences with God can help you see the problem more clearly and accept that He can't always show us what comes next. As Proverbs 3:5 says, "Trust in the Lord with all your heart, and lean not on your own understanding."

Relying on God's Strength and Support

God won't give you anything you can't handle. When you have a bad day, try to look on the bright side. Is there a lesson you can learn from a tough situation? Has going through a hard time made your relationship with God even stronger?

If you start to feel lost, remember that God is always there to support you. Reading the Bible, speaking to a religious leader, or praying can help you feel less upset about whatever is going on in your life. Whether stressed about a big project or upset about an argument with a friend, turning to God will remind you that you can get through anything with His love and understanding.

Dealing with Anger

When you're going through a tough time, you might even feel angry with God for letting something bad happen. From car accidents to hurricanes, there are all kinds of unpredictable events that can put people in harm's way. It's natural to be confused and wonder why God doesn't just stop these things from happening.

However, you also need to remember that God's plan is bigger than any single person or place. We don't know where we fit into that plan or what's going to happen in the future, but God does. Part of trusting God is accepting His wisdom without blaming Him or getting upset that things didn't go the way we wanted.

If you're having trouble with anger at God, it's a good idea to talk to someone about your feelings. A pastor or Sunday school teacher can help you work through your emotions. It's hard to admit you're upset with God, but being honest is also important. Sharing how you feel opens you up to healing and understanding.

CHAPTER EIGHT: CELEBRATING GOD

You don't need to go to church to celebrate God. Saying grace before you eat, praying at night, or writing down what you're thankful for are all ways to praise Him. Even if you're by yourself, you can still pray and work on your personal relationship with God whenever you want.

Holidays and special occasions give you the chance to celebrate with other people. These holy days connect Christians from different countries, cultures, and even time periods. Just think of how many people have celebrated Christmas or Easter in all of history.

CHRISTIAN HOLIDAYS

Christian holidays take place throughout the year. Some holidays, such as Christmas and Easter, are also celebrated by people who aren't Christians. Not everyone follows the same traditions and beliefs, so you may notice differences in how you celebrate major holidays compared to other kids you know.

Ash Wednesday and Lent

Lent begins on Ash Wednesday and lasts for 40 days before Easter. It usually starts in February or March. During Lent, Christians remember Jesus's sacrifice and the 40 days He spent in the wilderness before His death. Since Jesus didn't eat during this time, many Christians fast on Ash Wednesday and Good Friday, the day that Jesus was crucified.

Like other traditions, different denominations have their own beliefs. Catholics don't eat meat on Fridays throughout Lent; the only exception is fish. Many Christians also volunteer to give up something for Lent to honor Jesus's sacrifice. For example, you might stop playing your favorite game or give up drinking soda for 40 days.

Holy Week and Easter

Holy Week takes place during the last week of Lent. It starts on Palm Sunday, the day Jesus came to Jerusalem for the last time. His followers welcomed Him by waving palms. Christians celebrate Palm Sunday by folding blessed palms into crosses, waving palms during processions, and attending special church services.

Maundy Thursday is the day of the Last Supper when Jesus shared the First Holy Communion. Many Christians attend church on Maundy Thursday to take Communion. Some also wash each other's feet to remember how Jesus washed His disciples' feet at the Last Supper.

Good Friday takes place two days before Easter Sunday. Churches host special services on Good Friday to bring everyone together, and Christians reflect on how Jesus's sacrifice saved humanity from sin. Even though Good Friday is a serious occasion, it's also a time to show gratitude and thanks.

Churches often hold a vigil on the night leading into Easter morning. Easter Sunday marks the day that Jesus Christ was resurrected from the dead. Christians celebrate Easter and the promise of eternal life for all who believe in God.

Easter is a time of rebirth and getting a fresh start. You were probably baptized as a baby or a young child, but some people choose to become Christians after they're already adults. These new Christians may be baptized during the Easter Vigil. You might also see lilies around Easter celebrations since they're a sign of new beginnings.

Pentecost

Pentecost takes place 50 days after Easter. Jews and Christians both celebrate this time in different ways. For Jews, the holiday known as *Shavuot* marks the day Moses received the first part of the Hebrew Bible on Mount Sinai. It was originally also a festival to give thanks for the barley harvest.

In Christianity, Pentecost celebrates the day the Holy Spirit appeared to Mary and Jesus's closest disciples. The Holy Spirit gave them gifts and the ability to speak in other languages. When news spread of what had happened, a crowd formed to hear. Everyone was shocked to hear that Jesus's followers were speaking in so many different languages. They asked, "Aren't all these who are speaking Galileans? Then how is it that each of us hears them in our native language?"

Peter addressed the crowd and spoke to them about Jesus. Some people accused the Apostles of just being drunk, but Peter convinced the audience that it was the work of the Holy Spirit. He said, "Repent and be baptized, every one of you, in the name of Jesus Christ for the forgiveness of your sins. And you will receive the gift of the Holy Spirit." After hearing Peter's words, thousands repented and became new Christians.

Allhallowtide

In the West, Allhallowtide takes place between October 31 and November 2. It's a time of remembering the dead and all Christians who have passed on. It starts with All Hallows' Eve, the Christian name for Halloween. Churches often combine religious activities with the types of Halloween festivities observed by non-Christians. For example, your church might give out candy with a Christian theme or host a special service that includes Halloween activities.

All Saints' Day is celebrated on November 1. This holiday honors all the saints throughout history. It's especially important within the Catholic Church. On November 2, or All Souls' Day, we remember Christians who have died. Instead of going to church, Christians often go to the cemetery to honor loved ones.

Christmas

Christmas celebrates the birth of Jesus Christ to the Virgin Mary. Most families who observe Christmas have their own sets of traditions that get handed down from one generation to the next.

For example, your family might have a particular day that you take out your Nativity set and decorate your home.

Since schools and workplaces are usually closed around this time of year, you may have relatives visiting from out of town. This can be a great opportunity to introduce your loved ones to people in your congregation. If the opposite is true and you're traveling to a new place, you can experience another church and see how it's different from yours. Some churches host late services on the night of Christmas Eve, or you might attend together on Christmas morning.

CHRISTIAN FESTIVALS AND EVENTS

Christians also get together to celebrate God outside of formal holidays. These gatherings range from smaller local groups to international festivals. Events give Christians the chance to meet new people, pray together, and have fun. Your church might even sponsor trips to festivals or other events throughout the year.

Music Festivals

Music has always been an important part of worship. Your church probably has at least a choir and an organ. In recent years, other types of music, such as Christian rock, have become more popular. Songs in these genres still include lyrics that praise God, but the tunes sound more modern than the hymns you hear in church.

They might include drums, guitars, and even brass instruments like saxophones.

Christian music festivals have taken place all over the world. Germany hosts Christian Rock Night every year in December. Meanwhile, England's annual Greenbelt Festival started as a Christian music festival but welcomes people from every faith. New festivals pop up all the time.

In North America, the Christian Festival Association oversees events and keeps a list of shows.

A lot of Christian music festivals are open to kids. For example, Jesus People Campout in Michigan offers music, prayer, and activities for all ages.

Summer Camps

Attending summer camp is another option if you hope to meet other Christian kids and see new places around the country. A lot of youth ministries host their own summer programs, but you'll probably need to travel to find an overnight camp where you can get the full experience.

Christian summer camps combine the great outdoors with Bible study and prayer. You'll get to learn more about what it means to live according to God's teachings while hiking, swimming, and experiencing nature.

TRADITIONS AND RITUALS IN CHRISTIANITY

Christianity is full of traditions and rituals to celebrate God. Key rituals such as baptism will only happen once in your life, while others like Communion and Penance take place on a regular basis. The exact way you participate in traditions and rituals will depend on your church and the denomination you follow.

Baptism

Baptism frees us from sin and shows that we're followers of Jesus Christ. Christians can either be baptized by having water poured over their heads or going completely underwater in a body of water like a lake. Nowadays, most Christians are baptized as babies, but some adults accept Jesus later in life. As you've already learned, adults are usually baptized during Easter to celebrate their new lives as Christians.

Even Jesus was baptized. He found John the Baptist at the Jordan River and asked to be baptized as well. However, Jesus didn't have sins to wash away. For Him, it was a symbol of His obedience and dedication to God. Matthew 3:16–17 says, "As soon as Jesus was baptized, He went up out of the water. At that moment, heaven was opened, and He saw the Spirit of God descending like a dove and alighting on Him. And a voice from heaven said, 'This is my Son, whom I love; with Him I am well pleased.'"

Communion

If you haven't already had your First Communion, you've probably seen others going up to take Communion during services. Communion is a way of remembering Jesus's sacrifice when He died for our sins. The bread represents Jesus's body, and the wine represents His blood.

Matthew 26:26–28 describes the first Holy Communion at the Last Supper: "While they were eating, Jesus took bread, and when He had given thanks, He broke it and gave it to his disciples, saying, 'Take and eat; this is my body.' Then He took a cup, and when He had given thanks, He gave it to them, saying, 'Drink from it, all of you. This is my blood of the covenant, which is poured out for many for the forgiveness of sins.'"

The Bible doesn't say how often we should take Communion. Some churches offer it every week, while others only have Communion on special occasions. It's also common to require people to be baptized before they can take Communion.

Confirmation

Confirmation seals the relationship between you and God that first started when you were baptized. Since Christians are usually baptized as babies, Confirmation is a chance to fully accept Jesus and renew your commitment to God now that you're older. In denominations such as the Lutheran Church, you're only considered a full member after Confirmation.

Don't panic about your Confirmation. Your religious leaders will help you get ready and explain every part of the process. If you get stage fright thinking about being in front of everyone, just remember that this is a stage in every Christian's life. Confirmation is your opportunity to show your faith in God and celebrate with everyone in your church.

If you're Catholic, you'll choose a Confirmation sponsor. Their job is to guide you through the process of Confirmation from start to finish. Sometimes, one of your godparents will be available to serve as your sponsor, but any adult from your church can fill this role. When it's time for your Confirmation, your sponsor will present you to the bishop for anointing.

Penance

The Sacrament of Penance is an important part of the Catholic Church. Catholics confess their sins to a priest and express that they're sorry. The priest listens to their sins, gives them advice, and gives them a penance to show that they really want to repair their relationship with God. Penance is usually saying a certain set of prayers.

In other words, Confession is a way of receiving forgiveness. Catholics are required to confess their sins at least once a year, but most Catholics go more often. Kids usually have their First Penance when they're in second or third grade. If you're Catholic and you're worried about having to tell someone else your sins, remember that priests aren't allowed to share or repeat anything they've heard.

Other denominations besides Catholics confess their sins in different ways. Instead of individual Confession, some churches confess their sins as a whole congregation during a group prayer. Lutherans, for example, start out by saying, "Most merciful God, we confess that we are in bondage to sin and cannot free ourselves. We have sinned against you in thought, word, and deed, by what we have done and by what we have left undone."

Tithes and Offerings

Tithing involves giving one-tenth of your income to the church. These donations are a way to honor God's contributions to our lives. Not all Christians tithe, but some choose to do so. Others give money to the church through offerings. A collection plate is usually passed around during services. Your parents or guardians might even give you money to be able to put in your own offering.

Matthew 23:23 reminds us not to focus so much on tithing that we forget about other responsibilities. Jesus says, "Woe to you, teachers of the law and Pharisees, you hypocrites! You give a tenth of your spices—mint, dill, and cumin. But you have neglected the more important matters of the law—justice, mercy, and faithfulness."

PARTICIPATING IN RELIGIOUS CELEBRATIONS

Religious celebrations usually take a lot of planning. If you want to participate, talk to your church leaders and see what you can do. Even if you don't take a special role in every religious celebration, attending events and worshipping with the rest of your church is still important. It adds to the spirit of the event and shows that you're a dedicated member of the congregation. As you get older, you'll probably have more opportunities to help out and participate in a more active way.

Music and Art

Does your church have a youth choir? If so, you could join and perform for different church events. There may also be opportunities to play instruments or even lead a Sunday school performance. For example, you could volunteer to teach younger kids how to play simple songs using handbells or other basic instruments.

It's also common for churches to host caroling trips during the Christmas holidays. Singing carols in your community allows you to praise God and spread joy to others. You might go caroling through local neighborhoods or head to a nearby location like a nursing home to celebrate the miracle of Jesus's birth.

Theater

Youth groups often put on a Nativity play for Christmas. The play tells the story of how Jesus was born in Bethlehem. Angels appeared to the shepherds and said, "I bring you good news that will cause great joy for all the people. Today in the town of David, a Savior has been born to you; He is the Messiah, the Lord." The Three Wise Men also traveled to Bethlehem to bring the baby Jesus gifts of gold, frankincense, and myrrh.

If you enjoy acting, ask if you can sign up for the play. There are usually roles for people of all ages. Your church may also put on other shows throughout the year that focus on various stories from the Bible. Auditioning could help you discover a new passion that lets you express yourself and praise God at the same time.

Community Projects

Your congregation might host projects out in the community as part of religious celebrations. For example, many churches collect toys during Christmas to share with families in need. These projects allow you to spend time with your congregation while also helping others in your local area.

CHAPTER NINE: QUESTIONS KIDS HAVE ABOUT GOD

It's totally normal to have questions about God. There's nothing wrong with being curious, researching what you already know, and trying to learn more about your religion. It doesn't mean you're not faithful to God or not Christian enough. Asking questions just shows that you want to understand God on a deeper level.

When you read the Bible, look at how often Jesus's disciples asked questions. He never told them to stop or discouraged them from asking more. Jesus wasn't even upset when others questioned whether He was truly the Messiah. He understood that people would have doubts or needed convincing.

When King Herod threw John the Baptist in prison, John may have experienced doubt or felt unsure about everything Jesus had promised. He sent his followers to ask Jesus whether He was the one they were waiting for, but Jesus didn't answer directly. Instead, He performed miracles. In Luke 7:22, He says to John's followers, "Go your way, and tell John what things ye have seen and heard; how that the blind see, the lame walk, the lepers are cleansed, the deaf hear, the dead are raised, to the poor the gospel is preached."

COMMON QUESTIONS AND DOUBTS

All different kinds of people believe in God, but there are certain questions that come up more often than others. You may have already talked about some of these questions in small groups or Sunday school. Being honest about your doubts or fears can help other kids open up about their feelings. You never know when someone else is too shy to ask the first question or admit that they're confused.

Don't be ashamed if you have doubts. After the women visited Jesus's tomb and realized it was empty, they hurried back to tell the rest of His followers. Luke 24:11–12 says, "But they did not believe the women, because their words seemed to them like nonsense." Only Peter went to the tomb to see what had happened.

Later, Jesus appeared to his closest disciples. They were scared and thought they were seeing the ghost of Jesus. He said, "Why are you troubled, and why do doubts rise in your minds? Look at my hands and my feet. It is I myself! Touch me and see; a ghost does not have flesh and bones, as you see I have."

Jesus showed mercy to those who questioned the truth. He wasn't angry or upset with them for not believing the women. Instead, He used those moments to teach the disciples and give them instructions on how to preach the word of God.

Where Did God Come From?

Even though God made us and all the other creatures on the Earth, that doesn't mean something else created Him. God has always existed. He's been there since the beginning of time. Colossians 1:17 says, "He is before all things, and in Him all things hold together."

Why Doesn't God Intervene When Bad Things Happen?

Humans have free will, which means that some people make choices that hurt others. Just think about Adam and Eve eating the forbidden fruit. God could have stopped them, but He allowed them to decide for themselves. We ask God to forgive our sins because we aren't perfect, and we don't always do the right thing.

God also knows much more than we do. He has all the information to make decisions ordinary people can't understand. When something bad happens, it's for a reason. We have to trust in His wisdom and let Him guide us.

Did God Write the Bible?

The Bible is God's word. Instead of physically creating the Bible, He inspired humans to write down His messages. In Jeremiah 20:9, the prophet Jeremiah says, "His word is in my heart like a fire, a fire shut up in my bones. I am weary of holding it in; indeed, I cannot."

Ultimately, the Bible is God's word regardless of the humans who wrote it down. God used humans to share His rules and teachings. Many books are labeled with a person's name, but ones like Acts are left open-ended.

Who Goes to Heaven?

Christians who love God and accept Jesus as their savior will have everlasting life in heaven. Even though all of us have committed sins and broken some of God's rules, we still repent and ask for forgiveness. In John 14:6, Jesus says, "I am the way and the truth and the life. No one comes to the Father except through me."

Spreading the word of God makes sure that other people have the chance to hear the truth and embrace Jesus. Matthew 28:19–20 says, "Therefore go and make disciples of all nations, baptizing them in the name of the Father and of the Son and of the Holy Spirit, and teaching them to obey everything I have commanded you." This is why Christians often travel to other places to tell more people about Jesus's love.

Do Animals Go to Heaven?

The Bible doesn't say whether animals go to heaven. After all, animals aren't the same as humans. They don't have free will or the ability to believe in God. However, it could be possible. Remember that God created animals in the Garden of Eden just like He made Adam and Eve.

The Bible also tells us to be kind to other creatures. Proverbs 12:10 says, "The righteous care for the needs of their animals." We can't guess whether God has a plan for each animal after death, but many Christians hope they will one day be reunited with the animals they loved during their time on Earth.

Why Doesn't Everyone Believe in God?

There are almost eight billion people in the world, and every single person is on their own spiritual journey. You can't force people to believe in God if their hearts aren't in it. God wants us to follow Him of our own free will.

Throughout your life, you'll meet other people who have different religious beliefs. Some people don't believe in God because they're waiting for proof. Others follow different religions besides Christianity. A lot of people just aren't sure. They may still choose to become Christians later in their lives.

You can't change what another person believes, but you can always pray for them and ask God to guide them. If someone asks about your religion, feel free to share your thoughts and answer their questions. 1 Peter 3:15 says, "But in your hearts revere Christ as Lord. Always be prepared to give an answer to everyone who asks you to give the reason for the hope that you have. But do this with gentleness and respect..."

Hearing you talk about your faith or meeting members of your church could convince people to become Christians. That's why it's always important to set a good example and treat everyone with kindness, even if they don't believe in God.

HOW TO FIND ANSWERS AND SEEK GUIDANCE

One of the simplest ways to seek guidance is to talk to the religious leaders in your life. Your pastor, priest, or youth group leader can help you work through any questions or doubts. They can also show you different passages in the Bible or pray with you to ask God for guidance.

Your local library might have books on religion for kids. If you don't see any, ask the librarian to see what's available. Your Sunday school may also have handouts or other materials you can study to learn more about God.

While you're looking for answers, keep in mind that you won't be able to find them all. As humans, we aren't meant to know everything about God and His will. Trusting in God means having faith even if you can't prove what you know to be true from studying the Bible.

THE IMPORTANCE OF CURIOSITY AND LEARNING

Being curious encourages you to ask questions and keep learning. You never know what you might discover by talking with a friend or rereading parts of the Bible. Although learning is important when you're at church, there's also a lot to learn from everyday experiences. For example, spending time outdoors and looking up facts about nature can help you appreciate all of God's creatures.

Changing Your Mind

No one expects you to have everything figured out. Changing your mind is just a sign that you're open to new ideas. If you grew up going to church, you probably formed a lot of your opinions when you were very young. Now that you're older, it's okay to change your mind or have new ideas about what it means to be a good Christian. After all, if you ask the same question to a kindergartener and a sixth grader, you're probably going to get very different answers.

Encouraging Open Discussions About Faith

Small groups and Bible study give you a place to talk about God with other Christians. You don't have to agree with everyone else, but you'll still have many beliefs in common. If you don't feel like you can be honest, talk to the leaders you trust in your church. They can help get your Sunday school class or youth group back on the right track if it feels like others aren't welcoming.

Listening to Other Views

Talking to other people about their views and beliefs can help you see things in a different way. That includes asking tough questions and discussing serious issues such as sin. Remember to be respectful when someone else is talking about their beliefs. Just because they have a different understanding of a certain story or they don't agree with what you've heard in church doesn't mean they're wrong.

Respectfully Disagreeing

At some point, you'll have disagreements with others about your faith. Someone from your church might feel one way about a certain part of the Bible, while you're certain those passages mean something else. When you're stuck in a disagreement, there's no need to be rude or insist that you're right. Everyone is entitled to their own beliefs and opinions.

If another person has a different view, offer to study the Bible with them. They might be looking at a different verse than what you had in mind. Showing respect allows you both to learn from the other without hurting anyone's feelings.

CHAPTER TEN: GOD AND COMMUNITY

Christians have always formed religious communities to worship together. Before there were churches all over the world, early Christians would meet in homes, synagogues, or even lecture halls. It's still important to gather and spend time at church, but that's not the only way to stay in touch with your community.

In modern times, it's easier than ever to stay connected. You can text, call, or even video chat with one of your friends from church without having to leave home. Many churches have also started streaming their services live on the internet for members of the congregation who can't come in person.

THE MEANING OF FELLOWSHIP

Fellowship is about sharing and participating in worship together. It's more than just being friends or having beliefs in common. Christians who unite in fellowship see themselves as part of a group that can never be separated. Anyone who loves God and follows Jesus is part of this community.

The idea of Christian fellowship dates back all the way to the earliest days of Christianity. After Jesus ascended into heaven, Acts 2:44-47 tells us, "All the believers were together and had everything in common. They sold property and possessions to give to anyone who needed them. Every day, they continued to meet in the temple courts. They broke bread in their homes and ate together with glad and sincere hearts, praising God and enjoying the favor of all the people."

If someone from your church is in need, helping them honors the fellowship between all Christians. It shows that everyone who believes in God is part of the same family. During tough times, it can be reassuring to know that so many people truly love and care about you.

SERVING THE COMMUNITY

Jesus always looked for opportunities to serve others. He didn't look down on anyone or turn people away when they were in need. Even when Jesus left to be on His own after hearing about the death of John the Baptist, He wasn't angry to discover that crowds of people had followed Him. He healed the sick and fed all 5,000 people from just five loaves of bread and two fish.

Even though we can't perform miracles, we can still follow Jesus's example by serving the community. These acts don't have to be complicated. Putting others first could be as simple as inviting someone to sit with you at lunch if they seem lonely.

Helping for the Right Reasons

Acts of service are supposed to be selfless. You should try to help others because it's the right thing to do, not because you hope someone will notice. Just think about the difference between these two situations:

- Person A sees an old woman counting change and looking upset while she tries to buy the cheapest item on the menu at a fast-food restaurant. They go to the counter and give the woman some extra money so that she can afford a bigger meal. After they give her the money, they sit back down and quietly finish their food.
- Person B sees the old woman and starts recording a video on their phone. They make a show of going up to the woman and giving her the money. They also record her reaction and then post the entire video on social media.

In this example, Person A just wants to help because they noticed the old woman was having a hard time. They didn't expect any recognition or praise from others. Person B posts the video on social media because they want everyone to know they did a good thing. Did they really care about the old woman at all?

BUILDING FRIENSHIPS THROUGH FAITH

It can be incredible to have friends who support your faith and share your love of God. When it's time for celebrations or rituals, you'll automatically have friends who want to join in. You can also study the Bible or pray as a group when you're spending time together. Not everything you do has to be religious, but it's nice to know that you can still be open about your faith if there's something you want to talk about.

Making Friends at Church

Church is a great place to meet other kids your age, especially if you all go to different schools. Your Sunday school or youth group will probably look a lot different than your regular classes. Instead of only talking to people you already know, try going up to someone new and introducing yourself.

You never know when another kid is feeling nervous about joining a new church or fitting in with your youth group. Saying hi and introducing yourself can make them feel welcome. Even if you don't have anything else in common, you're both Christians who believe in God. That can give you plenty to talk about while you get to know each other.

Meeting Others in the Community

Volunteering with your church and participating in community events gives you the chance to meet other people in your area. As you see more of your town, you'll be able to form a deeper connection to where you live. Nowhere is perfect, but looking for the positives can help you find reasons to be thankful for your community.

Plus, you don't know where you'll end up once you're older. Around 42 percent of people move to a different state than where they grew up. Moving can be stressful at any age, but as long as you're close to a church, you'll already have somewhere you feel at home.

THE IMPORTANCE OF UNITY AND COOPERATION

Christianity has dozens of different branches. Each denomination has its own rules and traditions. Throughout history, Christians from different groups have fought and attacked each other. In fact, the Puritan pilgrims who first came to America on the *Mayflower* wanted to settle in a new place because of disagreements with the Church of England.

Nowadays, different denominations try much harder to get along. Even though everyone doesn't agree all the time, it's important to remember that we're all still part of the same Christian family. Trying to work together and show respect for other denominations has led to celebrations such as the Week of Prayer for Christian Unity.

Week of Prayer for Christian Unity

The Week of Prayer for Christian Unity is celebrated by churches all over the world. In the northern hemisphere, it takes place between January 18 and January 25. The southern hemisphere celebrates later in the year. It was started in January, 1908 just outside of New York City.

Many types of churches participate. For example, the Catholic Church, the Methodist Churches, and the Eastern Orthodox Churches are all involved despite having very different traditions and beliefs. The Week of Prayer for Christian Unity brings everyone together to celebrate God as one overall community of Christians.

CHAPTER ELEVEN: UNDERSTANDING OTHER FAITHS

There are thousands of different religions all over the world. Christianity is just one. Learning about other religions can help you understand more about other cultures, countries, and traditions. Researching major religions around the world is a great place to start.

When ranked by the number of followers, Christianity is the largest. Around 2.38 billion people consider themselves Christians. Greece, Venezuela, and Romania are just a few of the countries with a Christian majority. Some denominations are more popular in different parts of the world. For instance, most Venezuelans are Catholic.

Islam has the second-highest number of followers at 1.91 billion people. Countries with Muslim majorities include Algeria, Pakistan, and Iraq. Islam has two main branches: Sunni and Shia. Up to 90 percent of Muslims are Sunni.

Hinduism has approximately 1.90 billion followers. It's the most popular religion in India and Nepal, but countries such as Sri Lanka, the United States, and Indonesia also have large numbers of Hindus.

You don't have to stop once you've learned about the major religions with the most followers. Small and medium-sized religions still have rich traditions and histories, even if they don't have billions of followers. Shinto, Judaism, and Jainism are just a few to get you started. As you learn, you might be surprised by how much Christianity has in common with other religions from around the world.

LEARNING ABOUT DIFFERENT RELIGIONS

There are many ways to learn about other religions. You might study some of them in school or hear certain details about another religion mentioned on TV. If you have questions, ask your parents, guardians, or religious leaders to explain some of the differences between Christianity and other religions.

Asking About Someone Else's Religion

Hearing someone else describe their faith can give you a better idea of what it's like to follow that religion. However, not everyone feels comfortable talking about their religion. Even though you might be curious about someone's faith, it can be rude to suddenly ask personal questions. It's usually okay to ask your friend a question if they bring up their religion, but it's still a good idea to check first.

This could be as simple as saying, "Hey, is it okay if I ask something about your religion?" That way, the other person gets to decide whether they want to talk about it. If you ask a question without making sure the other person is comfortable answering, it might seem like you're pressuring them to respond.

Visiting Other Places of Worship

You won't always be allowed to visit other places of worship. It depends on the rules of that faith and the exact circumstances.

Some places of worship might invite guests for special occasions or celebrations only. If you aren't sure whether you're allowed to go, ask to make sure. You may also be asked to follow certain traditions of the other religion such as wearing a kippah/yarmulke while visiting a synagogue.

RESPECTING AND APPRECIATING DIVERSITY IN FAITH

Even though you don't agree with someone else's religious beliefs, you should always treat others with respect. In fact, the Catholic Church officially states that missionaries who hope to spread Christianity should create "a respectful dialogue with those who do not yet accept the Gospel." The church also points out that Christians can still learn from speaking to others by appreciating examples of truth and grace that can act as a "secret presence of God."

Loving Others as Jesus Loves Everyone

Remember that Jesus shares His love with everyone. Follow His example whenever you're around people of other faiths. Even though they aren't Christians, people who follow other religions still try to be honest, loving, and kind. As Christians, we should appreciate those values in others regardless of whether they're part of the same faith.

Supporting Friends and Loved Ones

Studies show that up to 20 percent of Americans were raised by parents with different faiths or denominations. The possibility of having a friend or relative who follows another religion is even higher. Celebrating their special occasions or attending religious rituals shows that you respect their beliefs. You might go to your Jewish friend's bar mitzvah or accompany your Buddhist aunt to the temple.

Similarly, it's usually okay to reach out to friends and loved ones who follow other religions to invite them to your events. In many cases, other faiths allow followers to visit churches as long as they don't participate in Christian rituals or prayer. If you're not sure, ask a trusted adult in your church or talk to the person you want to invite.

COMMON VALUES AND TEACHINGS ACROSS RELIGIONS

Other religions have their own ideas about God and what it means to be holy. However, you'll also find a lot of similarities. Most religions have a code of behavior that inspires believers to be good people and try to make the world a better place. For example, Buddhists value kindness, love, and compassion for all creatures. You don't need to look far in Christianity to find those same ideas.

Some other religions also believe in parts of Christianity. Muslims recognize Jesus as a messenger of God, and their holy book, the Quran, refers to Jesus as "Messiah." They don't agree that Jesus was the Son of God, but they do view Him as a prophet. Taking the time to learn more about other faiths can help you find these common areas.

HOW TO ENGAGE IN INTERFAITH DIALOGUE

Even though you're a Christian, there are thousands of other religions in the world. If you only talk to other Christians, you'll miss out on friendships and experiences that involve other faiths, cultures, and backgrounds. Having healthy relationships with all types of people makes it easier to work toward shared goals, such as achieving peace around the world.

Interfaith dialogue can happen at any level. It doesn't need to be part of an international event or a national movement. Your church can even host its own interfaith event to welcome residents from throughout your local community and form stronger relationships with people who follow other religions.

Making Decisions About Interfaith Harmony

In 2020, a group of rabbis met in Poland to talk about whether Christians should be allowed to pray in synagogues. Christians who wanted to understand more about Judaism had been asking to visit and learn more about Jewish traditions. The rabbis decided that Christians could pray in the synagogue and wear a cross as long as they were respectful. They believed that it was an important opportunity to connect with Christians and become friendlier to people from other faiths.

World Interfaith Harmony Week

We've already talked about the Week of Prayer for Christian Unity, which brings together Christians from different denominations. There are also events where people who follow entirely different religions celebrate all faiths.

In 2010, the United Nations created World Interfaith Harmony Week to promote peace and understanding between religious groups. The event now takes place every year from February 1 through February 7. Each year has its own theme to bring attention to a particular problem or idea.

CHAPTER TWELVE: GROWING IN FAITH

As you grow up, your faith will change as well. You'll face new challenges and questions as you experience more of the world. When your routine is suddenly different from going to a new school or joining your first sports team, you'll have to rethink your daily life. That includes figuring out how you feel about your faith and whether your relationship with God needs more of your attention.

When you're having trouble with your faith, think about what's holding you back. Are you afraid of the future? Are you upset about something bad that happened? Asking yourself these questions can help you see what you need to fix to become closer to God. If you're worried about a big change like going to high school, then reading the Bible or talking about your fears with your small group can remind you that God is always there to guide you through difficult times.

DEVELOPING A PERSONAL RELATIONSHIP WITH GOD

We all have our own personal relationships with God. It can be wonderful to worship as a group, but there's something special about connecting with God on your own. Maybe you see God whenever you spend time with your family and show love to your closest friends. Someone else might feel closer to God while they're in nature.

Try not to compare yourself to other Christians. There's no right or wrong way to love God as long as you're following His teachings and doing all you can to live a godly life. Some people might not agree with your habits and how you show your faith, but your relationship with God is as unique as you are.

Ways to Stay Close to God

This probably sounds obvious, but one of the simplest ways to stay close to God is to think of Him often throughout the day. When you keep God in your heart and mind, it's easier to see what God would want you to do in your daily life. If you get too distracted by school, activities, or socializing, you could end up making the wrong decision when it matters.

Making prayer a habit will also keep God in your heart no matter how much things change in your daily life. If you used to say your prayers before bed, but now you feel more connected to God in the morning, then go ahead and change your routine. Holding a place for God shows that you value your relationship with Him no matter what else you have going on in your day-to-day life.

Accepting God's Wisdom

God doesn't always answer our prayers if we're asking for something He doesn't believe is right. Just as you wouldn't stop loving your parent or guardian for telling you no, your relationship with God shouldn't be based on asking for blessings. There are times when God's plan is different from what we want.

Accepting His wisdom is part of maintaining a healthy personal relationship with God.

CONTINUING TO LEARN AND GROW SPIRITUALLY

No matter how many times you've gone to church or studied the Bible, you won't be able to learn everything there is to know about God. Everyone makes mistakes and sins against God from day to day. Use these times to grow into a better person and figure out how to avoid making the same mistake again.

A lot of growth is personal, but you can still learn from talking to other people. Instead of always going to the same group or Bible study, listening to different people can help you see new ways of understanding the same stories. Even if you don't agree with someone else, hearing their opinion helps you learn about other perspectives besides yours.

Being Honest About Your Flaws

When you admit to your mistakes and flaws, you're actually telling yourself what you need to improve to be a better Christian. Imagine that you're watching your favorite television show when your brother accidentally drops a plate and makes a huge mess in the kitchen. Instead of helping him, you pretend you don't notice because you don't want to pause your show. Was that the right thing to do? Is that how Jesus would want you to treat someone?

Once you realize you've made a mistake, do your best to own up to it. That could mean apologizing to your brother and making a promise that you won't act like that again. When you say your prayers, you can work through the situation in more detail while you pray. God is always there to listen and guide us on a better path.

Setting Goals for the Future

Some spiritual goals take time to accomplish. Setting goals for the future can give you something to work toward in your journey as a Christian. For example, maybe you want to eventually become a teacher's aide in Sunday school. Listing the steps to reach your goal allows you to see what you need to do now to set yourself up for success.

Working toward goals also encourages you to keep learning and growing over time. When you have something you want to accomplish in the future, you won't let yourself get distracted as easily by things that aren't as important.

If you like to make goals into a game, think about setting up a prayer challenge. These usually last for at least a few weeks. You choose a different topic to pray about for each day of the challenge. Your friends, Sunday school classmates, or family members might be interested in making suggestions. This way, you can learn about different ideas from the Bible and challenge yourself to pray in detail about topics you may not have thought about before.

EMBRACING NEW EXPERIENCES

Whether you've decided to join a ballet class or you're heading off to your first sleep-away camp, embracing new experiences allows you to challenge yourself as you get older. Growing up involves a lot of changes to your personal life and routine, so it's a good idea to try new things when you can. Being open to different activities and experiences will help you learn how to adapt.

Honing these skills makes it easier to embrace change, even when it's outside your control. You'll eventually change grade levels, learn how to drive, and get your first job. Besides these major life events, you'll also have smaller changes, such as buying new clothes or trying a meal you've never had before.

Trusting in God

Leaning on God's love and support can give you the strength you need to step outside your comfort zone. New experiences just aren't as scary when you trust God to watch over you. Proverbs 3:5–6 says, "Trust in the Lord with all your heart and lean not on your own understanding; in all your ways submit to Him, and He will make your paths straight." If something you tried didn't work out as expected, you can always pray about it later to process how you feel.

INSPIRING OTHERS THROUGH YOUR FAITH JOURNEY

Seeing your faith journey can inspire others to think about their own relationships with God. You never know when another person is questioning their beliefs or wondering whether they've chosen the right path. Watching God work through Christians just like you could be the reason another person chooses to join a church or return to God's flock.

Encouraging the People Around You

Rather than just waiting for others to hear your story, you should also encourage the people around you. If you can tell another kid in your youth group is having trouble with their faith, ask them if they want to talk about it. They might be searching for a friend who will listen without laughing at them or judging.

Sometimes, just being kind to others in your daily life can show them what it's like to embrace God's love. Helping someone else and trying to spread joy in your daily life can inspire people to think more about their own relationships with God and how they feel about their faith.

CHAPTER THIRTEEN: GOD'S PROMISES

God makes many promises in the Bible. Unlike humans who lie or don't follow through, God always keeps His promises. Psalm 146:6 says, "He is the Maker of heaven and earth, the sea, and everything in them — He remains faithful forever."

Promises help us have a stronger relationship with God. After all, many of us already make promises to show our love and commitment to other people. Just think about your parents or guardians. They promise to take care of you and make sure you have everything you need. There are also public promises that people make in front of each other and God. When two people get married in a church, they take vows and promise to love each other in the sight of God.

UNDERSTANDING THE CONCEPT OF PROMISES IN THE BIBLE

When you think back to the Garden of Eden, Adam and Eve broke their promises to God by eating the forbidden fruit. After that, there was sin in the world. God sent His only Son to die for our sins and create a new relationship between humanity and God.

One of God's most important promises is that anyone who believes in Jesus will be saved. His decision to give us free-will allows us to choose whether to honor our promises to God and live according to Jesus's teachings or not. As long as we keep our promises, God will ensure that we experience salvation through Jesus Christ.

God's Love for Humanity

Signs of God's love for us are throughout the Bible. God's promise to love us started when He made the first humans and continues to this day. Even when God has been angry with humans, He's never turned His back on us or abandoned us. 1 Chronicles 16:34 says, "Give thanks to the Lord, for He is good; His love endures forever."

Support and Guidance

God promises to look after us and support us through tough times. In Isaiah 41:10, He says, "So do not fear, for I am with you; do not be dismayed, for I am your God. I will strengthen you and help you; I will uphold you with my righteous right hand."

Whenever you're afraid or nervous, just think about God's promise. If you feel confused about which choice to make in a certain situation, it's reassuring to know that God is there to guide you. You can always take a quick moment to stop and pray. Reaching out to God for support can be especially comforting when you don't have the chance to talk to your friends or loved ones before deciding what to do next.

STORIES OF GOD'S PROMISES AND THEIR FULFILLMENT

Some of the most famous Bible stories show God fulfilling His promises. When you read these stories, you'll see that God often asks us to be patient. He doesn't always keep his promises right away. Sometimes, we need to trust in God and wait for the time He believes is best.

The Promise of Jesus

The Israelites had Saul as their first king, but he disobeyed God and refused to follow the Lord's commands. After Saul's death, God chose a humble shepherd named David to be the next king. God made a promise to David that appears in 2 Samuel 7:12–14: "I will raise up your offspring to succeed you, your own flesh and blood, and I will establish His kingdom. He is the one who will build a house for my name, and I will establish the throne of His kingdom forever. I will be His Father, and He will be my Son."

Before Jesus was born, an angel appeared to Mary to tell her of God's plan and deliver the message that she would have a Son. The angel told Mary that God's promises never fail. Through Jesus, God promised eternal life and salvation for true believers.

Noah's Ark

There was a time in the distant past when God was upset with all humans. They were distracted by evil and refused to listen to God's commands. Noah was the only one who was still faithful. God told Noah to build a giant ark that could hold two of each creature. It took Noah 120 years to complete the ark and collect one male and one female from every species.

God warned Noah that he needed to go to the ark with his family. Noah also brought his wife, his three sons, and his sons' wives. Once they were safe, God sent a storm that lasted for 40 days and 40 nights. It rained so hard that everything on the planet was covered in water. Only Noah and his family were safe.

After many months, Noah sent out a dove to see if it could find land, but the bird returned. When he sent it out again, the dove came back with an olive leaf. That's how Noah knew there was land somewhere in the distance.

Once Noah and his family were settled on the land, God promised Noah that he wouldn't need to worry about a flood happening again. In Genesis 9:11, God says, "I establish my covenant with you: Never again will all life be destroyed by the waters of a flood; never again will there be a flood to destroy the earth."

Abraham and Sarah

God promised Abraham that he would have as many children in his family line as there were stars in the night sky. God also told him that his descendants would be kings and inherit the land of Canaan. Abraham was confused about what God meant. He and his wife, Sarah, were both old and had never had a child together. They doubted God's promise since no one else had ever had children at their age.

God repeated his promise to them years later. Finally, when Abraham was 100 years old, and Sarah was 90, they had their son, Isaac. After turning 60 years old, Isaac fathered twins named Esau and Jacob. According to Genesis 28:14, God appeared to Jacob in a dream and said, "Your descendants will be like the dust of the earth, and you will spread out to the west and to the east, to the north and to the south. All peoples on earth will be blessed through you and your offspring."

The story of Abraham and Sarah shows why we need to trust in God's promises even if they seem impossible. God is capable of amazing wonders that we can't begin to imagine. In some cases, His promises may take years and years to fulfill. Abraham and Sarah only had one child together, but they still had countless descendants in later generations.

Years later, God spoke to Moses to fulfill His promise to Abraham. He said that He would free the Israelites from slavery under the Egyptians. In Exodus 6:8, God explains, "And I will bring you to the land I swore with uplifted hand to give to Abraham, to Isaac, and to Jacob."

But after God freed the Israelites, they rebelled against God and refused to obey His commands. As punishment, God let them wander in the wilderness for 40 years, and Moses never reached the land that God had promised to his ancestors. Instead, God chose Joshua to lead the Israelites out of the desert.

The Israelites' story reveals that God keeps his promises according to His own plan. Even though He first made a promise to Abraham, it took many generations before it was fulfilled. This lesson reminds us that we're all just playing our own small parts to achieve God's goals for the times ahead.

THE HOPE AND ENCOURAGEMENT FOUND IN GOD'S PROMISES

God's promises give us something to hold onto when we're going through hard times. Even if you missed a critical goal in your soccer game or your close friend is moving away, God is always there to offer love and support. It can also be reassuring to know that God is still in control of everything that happens. A single mistake or painful moment isn't enough to change the good things God has in store for us.

Hoping for a Better World

Bad things happen every day, and it can be hard not to question God's will when we know He has the power to stop them. Even if people who have hurt others seem to get away with it, remember that not all of God's promises are blessings. The Bible also contains stories where God promised to punish people who hurt others and did evil deeds. In Exodus, God warned Pharaoh that He would send plagues against Egypt until the Israelites were free from slavery.

God doesn't have the same sense of time. For us, a year seems like a long time, but God is eternal. He has the patience and wisdom to wait for the right time to act. He may take decades to make a change that ultimately creates a better world. Since we don't have the ability to see what's ahead or know what's taking place throughout the universe, we can't understand exactly what God intends.

KEEPING YOUR PROMISES

Promises are serious, so you shouldn't give your word unless you intend to keep it. Doing what you say is a part of being honest and showing that you're trustworthy. Whether you swear you'll clean your room or promise to help your friend study before a test, going back on your word hurts the people who believed you.

There are some exceptions if you can't help but cancel even though you did everything you could to keep your promise. Maybe you missed your bus, so now you can't help your friend study on the way to school. Mistakes happen, but try your best not to make promises unless you know you can follow through.

Making Promises to God

Think carefully before you make a promise to God. Ecclesiastes 5:4–7 says, "When you make a vow to God, do not delay to fulfill it. He has no pleasure in fools; fulfill your vow. It is better not to make a vow than to make one and not fulfill it." If you're not sure whether you're fully committed to your promise, then it's better not to say anything. God won't be upset with you if you need time to think through what's right instead of rushing into a promise you won't be able to keep.

This is another time that it's important to have a personal relationship with God. Don't let anyone else pressure you into making promises. Your relationship with God is individual and unique. If your small group or Sunday school class is making a promise together, think through whether you fully agree. Being honest with God matters more than following along with what everyone else is doing.

Sometimes, you'll be asked to participate in rituals and ceremonies such as taking Communion. If you don't understand a ritual, ask someone you trust to explain it to you in advance. This way, you'll know whether you're making any promises to God and what the ritual is supposed to mean.

CHAPTER FOURTEEN: GOD'S PLAN FOR YOU

God has a plan for all of us. He designed us to have different hopes, skills, and interests. Every person has their own role to play, and God guides us toward the paths we're meant to follow. In Isaiah 14:24, God says, "Surely, as I have planned, so it will be, and as I have purposed, so it will happen."

DISCOVERING YOUR PURPOSE AND CALLING

Most people find fulfillment in more than one area of life instead of having a single purpose. A doctor who feels called to help people might also find purpose as a parent or volunteer. Even if you already know what you want to be when you get older, your life will still consist of other things besides what you do for work.

Being open to new experiences allows you to consider different paths. If you never take care of an animal, play a sport, or sing in a choir, how will you know that your purpose doesn't relate to one of those activities? There are plenty of famous celebrities and businesspeople who only discovered their passions later in life. For example, Harlan Sanders, the founder of Kentucky Fried Chicken, was 65 years old when he started the restaurant chain we know today.

Therefore, you don't have to rush to find your purpose right away. You'll slowly find bits and pieces of what makes you happy and fulfilled. In addition to your faith, you already have friends, family, and community. That's a great start to help you navigate life and figure out your personal calling.

God's Gifts to You

As you get closer to making major decisions about the future, your relatives, teachers, and friends will probably have their own opinions about what path you should take. While you should still listen to what they have to say, you shouldn't choose a path that doesn't call to you just because everyone else thinks it's the right decision.

Think through your options and what you like to do in your free time. Do you have any special skills or passions? When you hear someone talk about natural talents and gifts from God, what comes to mind? It's okay if you can't answer these questions right now. Take your time, and try to be patient as you discover more about who you're meant to be.

Motivations and Distractions

As you learn more about yourself, the question you should ask the most is, "Why?" Answering that question will help you recognize when your motivations are pure. If you want to join the school orchestra because you love playing music, that's a wonderful reason to sign up. On the other hand, if your·reason is selfish, you probably need to rethink your choices.

You'll constantly encounter distractions and temptations that try to lure you away from what's most important. If you get too distracted by greed, pride, or selfishness, you may miss what's right in front of you. Maybe there was a chance to discover more about your calling, but you were too focused on joining clubs that didn't interest you just to fit in with your friends.

Luckily, there are always detours that will guide you back to where you belong. In Jesus's parable about the lost sheep, the shepherd doesn't give up when a sheep goes missing from his flock. God's love is the same way. When you make a mistake or start moving in the wrong direction, God will always be there to welcome you home.

HOW TO LISTEN TO GOD'S GUIDANCE

Praying and reading the Bible are two key ways to connect with God and seek His guidance. Maintaining a strong personal relationship with God allows you to open yourself up to His wisdom and listen for His voice. Remember that prayer is a conversation with God. If you only speak but don't stop to listen, you may miss an opportunity for God to reach out and guide you.

God's Presence

God is everywhere, but some Christians feel closer to God in certain places. One of the most obvious locations to connect with God is in church. If you're facing a problem or have to make a big decision, going to church could help you sort through your feelings. You don't even need to wait for a service. Even if no one else is around, you can still pray and sit quietly while you think.

Another option is to go outside and experience nature. Many people feel God's presence when surrounded by the world He designed. Whether you're watching the stars or enjoying the sun from your backyard, it can be inspiring to realize that everything in nature works according to God's plan.

Devotionals

Devotionals usually include passages from the Bible, an explanation of what you've read, or an exercise for you to think about. They're perfect if you want to read someone else's ideas or quickly learn about a few verses from the Bible. Devotionals can also help you pick out sections of the Bible to study later in greater detail on your own.

However, keep in mind that devotionals are made by other people. Their ideas about what a story or verse means could be different from yours. Try to form your own opinions about the Bible verses in devotionals instead of focusing too much on what others think. Completing exercises or answering questions from devotionals can make it easier to determine how you really feel.

MAKING DECISIONS WITH GOD'S HELP

When you need to make a decision, it can be beneficial to write out a list of pros and cons. Seeing the good and bad sides of each option will help you see which choice makes the most sense. As you're thinking about possible outcomes, you should also consider any stories from the Bible that talk about the issue you're dealing with.

Obviously, the Bible won't have details about modern technologies or the exact way our society works. At the same time, God's messages are universal and everlasting. There's always something in the Bible that can reassure you or show you how to lead a godly life. Instead of trying to solve a problem on your own, go back to the Bible and search for the verses that speak to you.

Follow Your Heart

It can be risky to listen to your heart instead of taking the time to really think through what God expects. The things you want won't always match up with God's teachings. If you don't think through each decision, you might end up talking yourself into something that strays from the path that God has set for you. Remember that Jeremiah 17:19 says, "The heart is deceitful above all things and beyond cure. Who can understand it?"

Imagine that your teacher accidentally dropped the answer key to an upcoming quiz. You find it, but no one else is around. You might be tempted to keep the answer key since it would help you get a better grade and convince your parents that you're responsible enough to go to Bible camp over the summer. At Bible camp, you'd be able to learn so much about God and your faith. Maybe it would even cancel out being dishonest this one time. When you think about it that way, keeping the answer key doesn't sound so bad.

This is just one example of how you can talk yourself into doing the wrong thing by focusing on what you want instead of putting God first. When you can, avoid rushing into major decisions and ask other members of your congregation for advice; they can help you see whether you're truly making a choice that honors God.

EMBRACING THE FUTURE WITH FAITH AND CONFIDENCE

Embracing the future doesn't seem as scary when you have faith in God and your own abilities. Even when facing a major life change, you don't have to do it alone. God is always with you, and you'll also have the support of your family, friends, and congregation. As a Christian, you're part of a global community of believers who take care of each other and share the love we receive from God.

Trusting in God's Love for You

When you feel uncertain about the future, concentrating on what you know for sure can help you feel more secure. For example, you'll probably be nervous on your first day of high school. You won't know much about the building, the teachers, or the kids from other middle schools. If you focus too much on the negative, you won't be able to look on the bright side. After all, you'll still have classmates you recognize from your former school to give you a sense of normalcy while you adjust.

Additionally, you can take comfort in the fact that God is watching over you. If you're afraid of change or the unexpected, remember that God is there to hear your prayers and guide you through it. Psalm 32:10 says, "Many are the woes of the wicked, but the Lord's unfailing love surrounds the one who trusts in him."

CONCLUSION

Congratulations on reaching the end of this book. Hopefully, you've learned a lot about yourself and your faith along the way. We started by discussing the concept of God and how He created the universe around us. From there, we talked about the importance of prayer, studying the Bible, and living a godly life. You also learned about how to celebrate God in everyday life and on special occasions such as Easter and Christmas.

You should now have a better understanding of what it means to be a Christian and how to dedicate yourself to God. As you've already discovered, every Christian has their own unique relationship with God. When you have a healthy connection with God, you'll be able to make decisions about your future and seek His guidance as you get older.

Do your best to keep listening, sharing, and reaching out to others. In addition to reading the Bible and praying, you can learn even more about your faith by spending time with other Christians. Whether you're going to church or attending a Bible study group, there are many different ways to interact with your congregation. Someone else's ideas and opinions could help you see a new perspective you wouldn't have found on your own.

No matter what else you take away from this book, remember that God loves you and designed you according to His plan. That's why every person you meet is special and unique in some way. Whenever you're searching for God's presence, take a look at the world around you and appreciate the beauty and diversity of God's creation.

Made in the USA
Monee, IL
18 December 2024

74288077R00075